BOMBERS

Valerie Bodden

CREATIVE ● EDUCATION

Published by Creative Education
P.O. Box 227, Mankato, Minnesota 56002
Creative Education is an imprint of The Creative Company
www.thecreativecompany.us

Design and production by Liddy Walseth
Art direction by Rita Marshall
Printed by Corporate Graphics in the United States of America

Photographs by Getty Images (Annie Griffiths Belt, Ross Harrison Koty, Robb Kendrick,
Petrified Collection, Stocktrek Images, SuperStock, Roger Viollet), iStockphoto (Gary Blakeley,
Breckeni, Check Six, Scott Fichter, Richard Gillard, John Gomez, Taylor Hinton, Andrew Howe,
Iurii Konoval, Robert Simon), Shutterstock (Awe Inspiring Images, Ivan Cholakov Gostock-dot.net)

Library of Congress Cataloging-in-Publication Data

Bodden, Valerie.
Bombers / by Valerie Bodden.
p. cm. — (Built for battle)
Summary: A fundamental exploration of bombers, including their speed and carrying capacity, history of
development, targeting systems and other features, and famous models from around the world.
Includes bibliographical references and index.
ISBN 978-1-60818-125-4
1. Bombers—Juvenile literature. I. Title. II. Series.
UG1242.B6B635 2012
623.74'63—dc22   2010054402

CPSIA: 030111 PO1447

First edition
2 4 6 8 9 7 5 3 1

BUILT for BATTLE

BOMBERS

Valerie Bodden

A large airplane flies high above an enemy country.

It has been in the air for almost a day.

Suddenly, it drops several big bombs. Then it

speeds away. This is a bomber!

★ Famous Bomber ★
Junkers Ju-88

COUNTRY

Germany

ENTERED SERVICE

1939

LENGTH

47.3 feet (14.4 m)

WINGSPAN

65.7 feet (20 m)

WEIGHT

13.9 tons (12.6 t)

FASTEST SPEED

292 miles (470 km) per hour

CREW

4

The Junkers Ju-88 could carry
more than 5,500 pounds (2,495 kg)
of bombs. It was the fastest German
bomber of the 1940s and could be
used to drop bombs day or night.

Bombers are big military planes that carry bombs. They drop the bombs on enemy weapons, buildings, and TROOPS on the ground. Most bombers fly through the air at 600 to 1,600 miles (966-2,575 km) per hour.

A bomber dropping bombs to blow up buildings on the ground

English Electric Canberra

COUNTRY

Great Britain

ENTERED SERVICE

1951

LENGTH

65.5 feet (20 m)

WINGSPAN

64 feet (19.5 m)

WEIGHT

13 tons (11.8 t)

FASTEST SPEED

570 miles (917 km) per hour

CREW

2

The Canberra was one of the first bombers with JET ENGINES. It could fly much higher than other bombers of the 1950s. The Canberra was used for 57 years!

Pilots first began to drop bombs from airplanes in 1911. They just threw the bombs out the open COCKPIT of the planes! Later, bigger and faster planes were built. They carried bigger bombs.

Most older bombers

had engines that used

blades called propellers

Today's bombers have four or more jet engines.

Most bombers have a body called a fuselage

(*FYOO-suh-lazh*), two wings, and a tail.

Some bombers, called stealth bombers, look

like a giant wing. Their shape helps keep them

hidden from enemy RADAR.

Bombers can be from 50 to 150 feet (15.2-45.7 m) long. From the tip of one wing to the tip of the other, some reach about 50 feet (15.2 m). Others reach 185 feet (56.4 m).

That is as long as two basketball courts!

Bombers use computers and SATELLITES to help them find their targets. Some of their bombs are guided by satellites. This helps them hit their target even at night or in bad weather.

Computers in a bomber (top); bombs hitting the ground (bottom)

Only a pilot flies on some bombers. Other bombers have a copilot to help control the airplane.

Some bombers have other crew members who watch for enemies and fire weapons. Most bombers do not have much room for the crew to move around the cockpit.

Bombers can fly very far to get to a battle.

If they need more fuel, they can get it from

another airplane while they are flying.

When a bomber reaches its target, the

BOMB BAY opens to drop the bombs.

A bomber called a B-52

getting fuel from

another airplane

Some bombers fly next to fighter jets.

The fighter jets shoot enemy airplanes

that try to attack the bomber. They keep

the bomber safe to fight another day!

Northrop Grumman B-2 Spirit

COUNTRY

United States

ENTERED SERVICE

1997

LENGTH

69 feet (21 m)

WINGSPAN

172 feet (52.4 m)

WEIGHT

80 tons (72.6 t)

FASTEST SPEED

530 miles (853 km) per hour

CREW

2

The B-2 Spirit is a stealth bomber shaped like a big wing. Its shape and a special kind of paint help keep the B-2 hidden from enemy radar.

GLOSSARY

bomb bay—a big area on a bomber where bombs are kept until they are ready to be dropped

cockpit—the part of an airplane or helicopter where the pilot and other crew members sit

jet engines—machines that move an airplane forward by pulling air in through the front of the engine and pushing it out the back

radar—a system that uses radio waves and computers to find objects such as enemy airplanes

satellites—machines that circle Earth in space; they can send pictures and information about where an airplane is and what is on the ground below it

troops—soldiers or other people who fight in a war

INDEX

WEB SITES

Sky-Flash: Military Bombers
http://www.sky-flash.com/bombers.htm
See pictures of bombers in action.

War Eagles Air Museum: Fun Stuff
http://www.war-eagles-air-museum.com/fun_stuff.php
Have fun with bomber games and coloring pages.

READ MORE

David, Jack. *B-2 Stealth Bombers.* Minneapolis: Torque Books, 2008.

Demarest, Chris. *Alpha, Bravo, Charlie: The Military Alphabet.* New York: Margaret K. McElderry Books, 2005.